Tucholsky · Wagner · Zola · Scott · Sydow · Fonatne · Freud · Schlegel
Turgenev · Wallace
Twain · Walther von der Vogelweide · Fouqué · Friedrich II. von Preußen
Weber · Freiligrath · Frey
Kant · Ernst
Fechner · Fichte · Weiße Rose · von Fallersleben · Richthofen · Frommel
Hölderlin
Engels · Fielding · Eichendorff · Tacitus · Dumas
Fehrs · Faber · Flaubert · Eliasberg · Ebner Eschenbach
Feuerbach · Maximilian I. von Habsburg · Fock · Eliot · Zweig
Ewald · Vergil
Goethe · London
Elisabeth von Österreich
Mendelssohn · Balzac · Shakespeare · Dostojewski · Ganghofer
Lichtenberg · Rathenau · Doyle · Gjellerup
Trackl · Stevenson · Hambruch
Mommsen · Tolstoi · Lenz · Hanrieder · Droste-Hülshoff
Thoma · Hägele
Dach · Verne · von Arnim · Hauff · Humboldt
Reuter · Rousseau · Hagen · Hauptmann · Gautier
Karrillon · Garschin · Baudelaire
Damaschke · Defoe · Hebbel
Descartes · Hegel · Kussmaul · Herder
Wolfram von Eschenbach · Dickens · Schopenhauer
Bronner · Darwin · Melville · Grimm · Jerome · Rilke · George
Campe · Horváth · Aristoteles · Bebel · Proust
Bismarck · Vigny · Barlach · Voltaire · Federer · Herodot
Gengenbach · Heine
Storm · Casanova · Tersteegen · Gilm · Grillparzer · Georgy
Chamberlain · Lessing · Langbein · Gryphius
Brentano · Lafontaine
Strachwitz · Claudius · Schiller · Kralik · Iffland · Sokrates
Bellamy · Schilling
Katharina II. von Rußland · Gerstäcker · Raabe · Gibbon · Tschechow
Löns · Hesse · Hoffmann · Gogol · Wilde · Gleim · Vulpius
Luther · Heym · Hofmannsthal · Klee · Hölty · Morgenstern · Goedicke
Roth · Heyse · Klopstock · Kleist
Luxemburg · Puschkin · Homer · Mörike · Musil
Machiavelli · La Roche · Horaz
Navarra · Aurel · Musset · Kierkegaard · Kraft · Kraus
Nestroy · Marie de France · Lamprecht · Kind · Kirchhoff · Hugo · Moltke
Laotse · Ipsen · Liebknecht
Nietzsche · Nansen · Ringelnatz
Marx · Lassalle · Gorki · Klett · Leibniz
von Ossietzky · May · vom Stein · Lawrence · Irving
Petalozzi · Knigge
Platon · Pückler · Michelangelo · Kafka
Sachs · Poe · Kock
Liebermann · Korolenko
de Sade · Praetorius · Mistral · Zetkin

The publishing house tredition has created the series **TREDITION CLASSICS**. It contains classical literature works from over two thousand years. Most of these titles have been out of print and off the bookstore shelves for decades.

The book series is intended to preserve the cultural legacy and to promote the timeless works of classical literature. As a reader of a **TREDITION CLASSICS** book, the reader supports the mission to save many of the amazing works of world literature from oblivion.

The symbol of **TREDITION CLASSICS** is Johannes Gutenberg (1400 – 1468), the inventor of movable type printing.

With the series, tredition intends to make thousands of international literature classics available in printed format again – worldwide.

All books are available at book retailers worldwide in paperback and in hard-cover. For more information please visit: www.tredition.com

tredition was established in 2006 by Sandra Latusseck and Soenke Schulz. Based in Hamburg, Germany, tredition offers publishing solutions to authors and publishing houses, combined with worldwide distribution of printed and digital book content. tredition is uniquely positioned to enable authors and publishing houses to create books on their own terms and without conventional manufacturing risks.

For more information please visit: www.tredition.com

Bremen Cotton Exchange 1872/1922

Andreas Wilhelm Cramer

Imprint

This book is part of the TREDITION CLASSICS series.

Author: Andreas Wilhelm Cramer
Cover design: toepferschumann, Berlin (Germany)

Publisher: tredition GmbH, Hamburg (Germany)
ISBN: 978-3-8491-8476-6

www.tredition.com
www.tredition.de

Bremer Baumwollbörse, Bremen.

FIFTY YEARS.

A period covering 50 years is sure to show to the surviving and the younger generations certain milestones, which indicate a trend of human thought, or memorize important occurrences. We may look back upon mighty wars, or religious upheavals or the cruelties committed in both, or another may recall the peaceful thrifty life with its underlying romantic thought.

Later generations may possibly call this episode of the last 50 years the Period of Economic Development. Every epoch has its dominating spirit; sometimes it is a God of War, sometimes a religious martyr, sometimes it takes the shape of a great poet and even the thoughts and lives of the every-day citizen are the replica of the spirit of its time.

The embodiment of the spirit of the last 50 years is a Hercules. This famous demi-god executed 12 wondrous deeds, the names of which were painfully instilled into us at school, but his mighty deeds made no impression on the history of his time. Our Hercules has successfully achieved more than twelve wonderful works, nor need we look far afield to see the lasting imprint of his footsteps; we have always before us the great works of our time.

We are the lucky ones, who are privileged to step anywhere on our northern shore into a carriage, far more commodious than the ancient stage coach, compose ourselves for sleep, and allow ourselves to be whirled away, in order to find ourselves the following noon, seated at a comfortable meal on the heights of the Rigi. We have crossed the Atlantic Ocean in six days, we talk and listen to a friend, and it is nothing to us that he is a thousand kilometres distant. By pressing a button, we illuminate our house, by pulling a lever, we light up a whole town. From the birds we have purloined the art of flying, and many other wonders have the past fifty years showered upon us, and yet, all this is not the real monument of our time, but it is

"WORK!"

That systematic work, which is sure of its own goal, is the origin of all the wonders of the past half century, and which has set its own seal upon the special character of our own time.

If we consider the life of animals and even plants, we find that all adapt themselves to the demands of nature. This is the original primitive condition. But already the bird building its nest for greater comfort and protection of its young, interferes with nature's original conditions. No doubt, mankind once lived under primitive adaptation, and possibly the idealistic thought of paradise may be the echo of those far away days. When, however, mankind began to people the earth, necessity drove them to assist nature and thus "WORK" was created. For a long period this work was infinitesimal, and many races could still live from nature's storehouse. Their wants were few, so that the thought of exploiting nature for the benefit of improved conditions, never entered their heads. For forty years, Moses traversed the desert with the people of Israel, searching for gifts from Heaven, but they did not know, that--he who wishes to live upon milk and honey--must work to obtain them. By degrees, people began to try and win more from Dame Nature than she was willing to give unaided. They were forced, thereto, by their ever increasing numbers and by the individual demands on life. This healthy thought for improvement was frequently interrupted and, temporally, even entirely suspended, for in the human mind dwell not only great and lofty thoughts, but envy, strife and hatred have also a place. The history of mankind bristles with ugly deeds, wars, enslaving of nations and even extermination. Entire periods know nothing of peaceful development, but quietly and persistently "WORK" gained ground and forced itself, despite resistance, upon mankind. Only the more modern times have shown us the might and the blessing which lies dormant in "Work". Like an avalanche, the knowledge swept fifty years ago across the people, that quite different means were required for mutual benefit and culture, than those provided by nature itself. That was the triumphal entrance of "Work" towards a definite goal.

Words fail to adequately describe what the last fifty years have brought us, in inventions and kindred achievements, and what is the result of this Herculean work? An expansion undreamt of in the annals of history. By 50% the population of several countries had increased, they became too small to feed and clothe their people from their own resources, but the new spirit, which dominated all, has solved this problem, and great blessings have been vouchsafed to humanity. The "hard at work" countries had much better food, clothing, health and enjoyment, and each individual shared in the vast improvement of the general conditions of life.

What are the driving forces which put this gigantic machinery into motion? To enumerate them all would be impossible. The workman, who wields the hammer, the woman, who keeps home and hearth bright and cheerful, the patient teacher who moulds the juvenile mind, the professor, who disperses the deeper knowledge of science, the engineer, with his intricate machinery, the inventor, with his fertile brain, and, last not least the merchant, who constantly opens new roads for the interchange of goods, all--and every one of them are cogs in the wheels of the engines of progress.

The laws and rules which govern this world of activity cannot be determined. Each single one of the co-workers has the purpose and goal of his own endeavour before his eyes, but the human mind is incapable of guiding or even viewing, the concentrated action of all the forces at work.

We have given a cursory glance at the general economic development which started in the slowest possible way, and marched with double quick speed during the last fifty years, but now we shall turn to our own particular sphere.

We celebrate, to-day, the fiftieth anniversary of the Establishment of the Bremen Cotton Exchange, and with this book of sketches and sidelights on what we have felt and experienced, we wish to contribute a small offering to this festivity.

COTTON.

Cotton grows in almost every part of the Globe where the climatic conditions are favorable. The plant requires a moderate amount of moisture, but a good deal of sunshine and also warm nights. Countries with a moist warm climate are suitable for the raising of particular good qualities.

The chief country of production is the southern part of the United States of North America. Considerable crops are also grown in East India and Egypt, and lesser quantities come from the Caucasus, Turkestan, China, Brazil, Argentine, Peru and Africa. The continental consumption looks for the greater part to American cotton, but, also, East Indian is extensively used. In the Southern States of America, the first cotton ripens in August. The bolls containing cotton, will grow well into the Autumn, and even in Winter new bolls will be formed, and it is only a killing frost, which terminates the productive force of the plant. When the bolls are ripe, they open, and then the picking commences. As a rule, the first pickings are the best as to color and cleanness, and the longer the bolls are exposed to the inclemencies of the weather in Autumn and Winter, the more the quality will deteriorate. The picked cotton consists of two thirds of seed and one third of actual cotton. In order to obtain the fibre, the cotton is passed through a ginning machine. From the seeds, edible oil is gained and the residue is manufactured into food for cattle, while the cotton is formed into bales in specially constructed presses. It is natural, that cotton should show a great diversity of quality, owing to the influence of weather during the long period of picking. The color of cotton covers a fair range, one sees not only snow white and creamy cotton, but also bluish, grey, red and mixed colors.

The value of cotton is determined by its quality and character. Of chief importance is the percentage of the loss during the cleaning process in the cotton mill. A normal percentage of loss for medium grades is 10% , this is likely to be higher, if the cotton has been picked during moist weather and contains much unripe cotton. The color is also of great importance, discolored cotton has a decidedly lower value, especially when this cannot be rectified by bleaching which is mainly the case with heavily spotted or bluish cotton. An even greater factor, than the outward appearance, is the inner value, which is represented by the length and strength of the fibre (staple). The staple length of common American cotton is from 24-28 mm. In great request are the qualities, which have a longer staple than 28 mm, especially when the staple is even, silky and strong. A difference of only 1/2 mm in the length of the staple, may mean a difference of 10% in the value. It is of the greatest importance to the cotton merchant as well as to the spinner, that the cotton is correctly judged as regards its outward appearance and the length of staple, this adjudication or classing is by no means an easy task. A certain system has been adopted by which the outward appearance of the cotton is fixed by so-called standards into classes. A certain number of cotton samples are arranged in a suitable flat box, in such a way that their surface represents the color and cleanness of the respective class. If a lot of cotton is to be classed, samples are drawn from every bale, these are placed together, sample by sample, and the total thus gained, is compared with the standard. In this way an opinion is formed, whether the cotton is equal to the class represented by the standard, or whether it is below it, in which case, this difference in class has to be valued. The judging of the staple is a very difficult task, 1/2 mm is of importance, and yet it is impossible to measure staple correctly. Anybody, even with the greatest dexterity in his fingers, will not be able to draw from a piece of cotton the single fibres, place them in such a way next to each other, that they appear like Swedish matches in a box. A good expert, however, is able to draw the staple in a manner, that the average length will be accurately judged. To give a correct opinion on cotton, rooms with a good light are required, much experience and good judgment.

Next in importance for continental consumption is Egyptian and East Indian cotton. The former is divided into two kinds, the long stapled, which grows on the lower Nile, the Delta, and the shorter stapled, Upper Egyptian cotton. The long stapled Egyptian is utilised for the very finest yarns, and its only rival is or was Sea-Island cotton. This latter grows on a group of islands, not far from the shore of Georgia which have a moist warm climate, but the boll-weevil has played serious havoc with that crop, and the cultivation has been greatly curtailed. East India produces shorter stapled descriptions of great variety, but each has a character of its own, and yet to differentiate between them, is a knotty problem, especially, as now and then, one comes across a somewhat fraudulent mixture. The names are mostly derived from the locality in which they grow, while the climate and condition of the ground give the character, and in some cases, even distinctive smell, for instance, Oomra cotton smells like musk; occasionally the smell is an indisputable proof of origin.

It has taken the continental cotton industry a long time to grow from small beginnings to its present importance. The never lacking competition has brought about a great improvement in the quality and variety of the articles produced. It is astounding to compare the raw material in the fields, with the finished articles in the windows of some lady's outfitting shop. It requires many diligent hands and high class technical guidance, to transfer Nature's present of raw cotton into the manifold articles, which the people, nowadays, require and desire.

The variety of these articles is countless: cloth, as fine as a spider's web, and coarse fustian, here finest batiste, and there, strong drill for overalls. Each finished article requires its own particular raw material, low qualities cannot produce fine goods, and it is also impossible to utilise high qualities for low grade goods. The very arbitrary law for economic production, makes it a duty for every spinner to select just that quality of cotton, which is most suitable for his purpose, and it is the task of commerce to adapt the offers and deliveries to the requirements of the consumer.

THE OLD TIME.

In the year 186.., in the old narrow office, father and son met, the latter, a newly made partner. He had been, according to ancient custom, a volunteer for several years in London, where he had been well received amongst English families. But it was with strange feelings that he entered his father's office for the first time after many years of absence.

His horizon had widened, while here, little or nothing was changed. The old office furniture, which had done good service for generations, was the same, as no merchant ever thought of altering anything for merely a greater personal comfort, but the old fashioned standup desks and the well worn leather seats of the high office stools, did not look as inviting as of old. His memory had mellowed and idealized their appearance. Of course, the influence of the mother was not permitted in the sacred precincts of the office, even most of the cleaning was done by the youngest apprentice. But from the grey walls looked down proudly, the models of the sailing vessels which carried their houseflag to distant shores. During the long hours of a voyage, they had been fashioned by captains or clever sailors, and were a constant reminder of deeds nobly done.

Here is the "Anne Marie", a tea clipper of graceful lines, like a swallow, which made the journey from China to London in 80 days, and had earned, besides a good freight, a high premium for bringing the first tea of the new crop to the epicures in London. There is the "Katharina", much heavier in build, she took 180 days to fetch wet sugar and hemp from Manilla. One may wonder, whether captain and crew ever thought of the enjoyments of life, while they ploughed the sea for 6 months. Yonder, in the full light from the window is the "Nordstern", a whaler, and underneath a picture of the crew. These wild and rough fellows took their lives in their hands, on the perilous journey from Honolulu to the Polar Seas. They had no regular wages, but shared in the profits from the sale of the oil and whalebone. Their hard earned money, however, was mostly dissipated in San Francisco, during a few days of riotous jubilation.

After some desultory talking, the son carefully broached the following subject: "There is the "Augusta" ready in port to sail for Baltimore, to bring a cargo of tobacco. Pity, that the heavy Kentucky barrels fill only half the freight room and leave so much space empty. I think, father, we ought to fill it up with light goods, principally with cotton."

"Cotton, my dear boy! I fancy, you must be dreaming of the old firm of B. & F. You remember, F. told his agent, in the West Indies, to add to the cargo of Asphalt and cocoanuts, 200 bales of cotton. His bad handwriting led to the mistake that 2000 bales were shipped, the moment they were afloat, the Southern Ports were blockaded, which caused an unprecedented rise in the price of cotton, so that the last of the 2000 bales were sold at "one Thaler" per pound (equal then to three marks)."

"I do not think, father, that such luck is likely to repeat itself, but the fact remains, that we have room empty, which easily might carry freight, besides, I hear, that there is an increasing demand for cotton, as several new cotton mills are being started in Germany."

"Yes, that is all very well, but think of the enormous risk of the cotton trade. The fluctuations in prices are fabulous, recently, they have been going down and down. My friend W. has been holding cotton for 3 years and has never seen his price back yet. A loss he will not take, he declares 'that he will hold that cotton till he is black in the face.'"

"That is a wrong policy, W. ought to have sold the cotton long ago, replaced the same by a lower priced purchase, this would have saved him charges and loss of interest, and would have cheapened his original purchase."

"This is a new method of doing business, we--old Bremen people--stick firmly to an enterprise, until the success is secured. That is the old Hanseatic spirit."

"One might almost call it stubbornness, the present time requires quick thinking and turning."

"All right, but from whom will you take the money which is required by this modern way of doing business? The local money-broker has no spare cash for it."

"No, father, but I can assure you, that in London people are not adverse to assist the legitimate trade, and besides, several of the great London Bankers come from this neighbourhood and are very well disposed towards Bremen."

The "Augusta" brought, besides her cargo of tobacco, 1038 bales of cotton, quite a big quantity for that time.

QUESTIONS OF LAW
IN THE PAST.

According to the Universal German Commercial Law, and later, according to the Civil Code of Law, the buyer has the right to cancel the contract, or to demand a reduction in price, if the goods delivered do not equal the quality guaranteed.

Experts had to decide, whether the quality tendered was up to the guarantee.--These experts were appointed by the law, in accordance with the proposals of the parties concerned. The cotton trade followed, in olden days, this same procedure, but the weak point, was the verdict of the experts, because there were no experts in Germany outside Bremen, and no party could forecast the likely result of the verdict. A far worse consequence of the Law Conditions was for the cotton trade, the fact, that the law made no difference, whether the goods differed much or little from the stipulated quality. In both cases, the buyer had the right to place the goods at the disposal of the seller. The result of this, was most damaging to the Trade, sometimes, the sellers had the worst of it, sometimes the buyers. A few examples taken from actual experience will best explain this:

Extracts from business letters
of past years.

We have received to-day your 100 bales of cotton, but find the quality not up to our expectations. You have to deliver us middling-fair, but the cotton is hardly goodmiddling. We cannot use the cotton, as it is unsuitable for our hosiery yarns. We place the 100 bales at your disposal.

We insist upon your taking delivery of the 100 bales. The quality is perfectly correct, you can ask any expert in Bremen about it.

We have nothing to do with your Bremen Experts, if need be, our local experts will decide. We have no doubt that you know the law on this point. The fact remains, that we place the 100 bales at your disposal.

Your intention to place the 100 bales at our disposal is caused, no doubt, by the fall in prices. We know very well that if it comes to law, experts will decide, who know nothing about it, moreover, the verdict will only be given after many months. This is unbearable; what allowances do you want?

If you wish us to use the cotton, we demand an allowance of....

Your demand is preposterous, but we have to agree to it, as we cannot help ourselves. We prefer not to make you any offers in future.

I am sorry to inform you, that the 100 bales are not equal to the sample, consequently, I place the cotton at your disposal.

The buying sample has been taken from the actual bales delivered, a difference in the quality is quite impossible. We insist upon your keeping the 100 bales.

I am sending you a few samples of the delivered cotton, any child can see that they are different from the buying sample.

The samples sent to us are of no account. 100 bales represent a big quantity of cotton, amongst which, a few inferior flakes are sure to be found, if one searches diligently for them. We cannot agree to your demands.

My lawyer tells me, that every bale and every part of the bales must be equal to the sample. I have opened several bales and find the contents very irregular. There are good and bad flakes in them, I can only use regular cotton. The 100 bales are at your disposal.

Your 100 bales turn out very badly indeed and are much below the guaranteed quality. What allowance are you willing to make us?

There can be no question of an allowance, if the 100 bales do not suit you, why do you not place them at our disposal, as you did in a previous case. This time, however, prices have advanced, while last time, they had fallen, now perhaps the case will appear to you in a different light.

You surely never expect me to take bad cotton instead of good? I cannot return the cotton, as I cannot stop my mill. I propose, that experts fix the lower value, and you pay me the difference according to law.

If you wish to invoke the law, you must remember, that the cotton is not allowed to be touched, till the experts have made their report and the legal verdict has been given. You say, "you must use the cotton at once," while our agent tells us, "that a few bales have already been spun." This finishes your claim, and we refuse to do anything in the matter.

A spinner bought direct from America 100 bales of a certain class. The market rose rapidly, and when the bales arrived, they were much inferior, in fact, fully two classes too low. The spinner complained bitterly to the shipper, and demanded an allowance, which the latter refused, on the plea, that, for the price of the contract, he could only deliver low quality.

From these examples it will be seen that the cotton Trade had no suitable foundation in the Law.

ORIGIN OF THE BREMEN
COTTON EXCHANGE.

During the war of 1870/71 the cotton trade had suffered a serious relapse, but shortly afterwards, the Bremen people began seriously to consider means and ways to put the trade on a proper footing.

The industry had expanded, and the occasional chance business had been replaced by a more regular and closer connection with the spinners. The main thing to do now, was to find a proper basis upon which a regular market could be built up. The various questions of law had to be adjusted in a broad minded manner, to suit the particular need of the cotton market. Liverpool offered a good example for this, as there, everything had been adapted to the peculiarities of the cotton trade.

Here, in Bremen, first of all, the credit system had to be abolished. It was manifestly impossible to increase the import, as long as the importer was obliged to sell the cotton on 3-4 months open credit.

A good stock of cotton is the first necessity for a market of any importance, but how to obtain it, if the needful capital is lacking to pay for the cotton? The risk of the great price fluctuations, which are indigenous to cotton, gave the whole trade a bad name, and everybody, who had anything to do with it, lost prestige.

Was it worth while to follow up the idea of starting a cotton market?

We must praise the men, who made it practically their life's work, to overcome the difficulties, and must admire the cleverness with which they left certain items for the future to solve.

The men who laboured hard for this object, formed themselves into the "Committee for the Bremen Cotton Trade", later on, the name was changed, and on the 1st of October 1872, everything was ready, and under the new name of

"Bremer Baumwollbörse"

an organisation was started, which has since become known all over the cotton world.

On the 1st of October 1922, its birthday re-occurs for the fiftieth time.

Political occurrences make a deeper impression than those which fall into the sphere of National Economics, but the present has taught us, that the latter are by no means to be despised, in fact, deserve more attention than was given to them previously. It may be worth while to recall, that through the influence of the "Bremen Cotton Exchange", a well regulated trade of first magnitude has been built up. We are forced to observe the development of national economy, not only in our own country, but also, that in foreign countries, and by keeping the important factors constantly before us, we can learn a good deal.

ARBITRATIONS AND
APPEALS.

The department of the "Bremen Cotton Exchange" which deals
with questions relating to actual cotton, has a staff of sworn classers.
It is their duty to fix, with the aid of the various standards, the class
of cotton, or to pronounce an opinion on it, or to settle the disputes
between buyer and seller, as far as they refer to the quality of cotton.

American cotton is divided into a number of classes, and each has
its standard. Originally, these standards were obtained from Liverpool, but later on, Bremen produced the standards independently.
There are original standards and standard copies; the former, remain unchanged, while the latter are renewed every year, because,
through constant use, they are liable to deteriorate. The freshly
made up standards are subject to the examination and approval of a
Committee, elected for that purpose, and which consists of Members of the Trade and the Industry. The sworn classers are nominat-
ed by the directors, and concern themselves solely with the classing
and arbitrating of cotton. They have sworn a solemn oath, to con-
duct their office with absolute impartiality; this is further safe-
guarded by the fact, that the names of the parties interested are kept
strictly secret. If a party consider, that they have a right to complain
about the verdict of the classers, they can appeal against the decision. The verdict of the appeal is given by Appeal Judges, who are
appointed by a Committee, elected for that purpose. They are selected from the merchants and spinners, and great care is exercised
that they possess the necessary expert knowledge. The names of the
interested parties are also withheld from the appeal judges, nor are
they informed whether buyer or seller have appealed. It is of great
advantage to the whole arbitration system, that the appeal judges
are actively engaged in the cotton business, by this means a bureau-
cratic verdict is avoided. Up to a point, the arbitrators and appeal
judges work together, and thereby, the former remain in close touch
with the general business life, which is of importance for various
reasons. It is not sufficient for a correct verdict, to simply compare
the cotton with the standards, the judges must know, how the difference in the quality is to be valued; and how far the character of
each crop is to be taken into consideration, etc. etc. It is therefore

apparent, that the judging of cotton requires a certain connection with the actual business activity, and, it is certain, that only the commerce itself can produce and educate the individuals, who are chosen to pronounce an expert opinion upon questions of such importance and difficulty.

The "Bremen Cotton Exchange" does not only decide questions concerning quality, but settles also all other disputes, which may arise between members. These decisions are given by, what may be called, a court of arbitration and a court of appeal. To the former each party appoints its own expert, while the Exchange appoints the experts to the latter. The conditions of the "Bremen Cotton Exchange" are adapted to the common law, but take into account, the decided peculiarities of the cotton trade.

The following is an explanation of an important point, where the conditions differ from the Common Law. A deviation from the guaranteed quality, does not give the buyer the right to cancel the contract. He is awarded an allowance, when the difference is small; if the inferiority be greater, penalty is added to the allowance, but, when a heavy allowance is not likely to compensate the buyer for the damage sustained, he may return the cotton, but not by cancelling the contract. In such cases, the contract will be what is called, "regulated" or "invoiced back", in which method, the market differences are duly taken into account, with the addition of penalty for the guilty party. When sales are made for specified deliveries, and these should not be made within the proper time, the buyer has also the right of invoicing back, in the manner described. This invoicing back, takes the place of the cancelling of a contract, according to law.

It is possible, that when a party practically goes by default on a contract, through a very inferior tender, or by a late delivery, they may yet be entitled to claim from the other party, a difference in price. For instance: Somebody sells cotton at 22 cents, the market drops to 20 cents, the contract is invoiced back for bad delivery, then, the seller, who is the guilty party, has a claim against the buyer, for a difference in the market of 2 cents less penalty of 2% = 0.44 cents, equalling 1.56 cents net.

This claim would not be possible according to Common Law. The conditions of the "Bremen Cotton Exchange" make it a principal, that no party shall take an advantage of the market fluctuations.

In the above case, the buyer would have a profit of 2 cents, if he could have simply cancelled the contract on account of bad delivery, because he could have immediately re-bought the cotton at 20 cents, while all his calculations were based on a purchase at 22 cents. This apparently strange fact, that the innocent should pay to the guilty, is the direct consequence of the elimination of market fluctuations from the Law Codes.

It has been of great benefit to all concerned, that any differences of opinions are promptly settled by the "Bremen Cotton Exchange", and not by having resort to a costly and wearisome law suit. Everybody in cotton knows, that quarreling is always bad business, and, it is with some pride, that the cotton Exchange looks back upon the big number of decisions given.

Only very rarely has it happened, that disputes have been referred to the ordinary Law Courts. The "Bremen Cotton Exchange" has, according to the Rules, the power to do so, but that right is only exercised, where purely matters of Law are concerned.

THE UNION
WITH THE INDUSTRY.

The Bremen Cotton Market made slow progress and now and then the progressive movement was interrupted. It required courage to pursue the projected course, but "never despair" was the motto which finally carried the day. It became apparent, that the "weal or woe", of the market depended upon the attitude of the Industry. Far sighted men strove hard to awaken an interest for Bremen amongst the spinners, who still utilised considerably the Liverpool market.

The following letters bear witness how this idea was received:

Bremen, ... 1886.

The time has arrived, when the South German Cotton Industry should decide to come a step nearer to the sea. Frequently, complaints have been made about mutual misunderstandings, and that this lack of understanding had given rise to friction. If the spinners would unite with the Bremen cotton trade, an opportunity would be created for eliminating these misunderstandings. By talking matters over in a friendly spirit, and becoming known to each other, common interests could be defended and furthered. There is no danger that the spinners might be outvoted in Bremen, for there is a strong feeling here, that the common welfare must predominate, and that the Bremen trade depends, to a large extent, upon the goodwill of the Industry.

Augsburg, ... 1886.

We note with pleasure the suggestions, which we received from you verbally, and by letter, and are convinced that the reasons which you advance for a union with your market, are perfectly correct. Many of our spinners are a little out of the world, and it would be of advantage to them, to come into closer touch with the foreign and oversea trade. We shall gladly come to Bremen, after the necessary arrangements have been made in Augsburg. We do not wish to be merely affiliated, but desire to become active workers; for this purpose, we should require full membership, with voting power. We shall take care that Bremen--as a German Sea Port--attains the position in the cotton World, which it deserves.

In July 1886, the entry of the German Spinners into the "Bremen Cotton Exchange" became an accomplished fact. The arrangements, which the trade had made, for dealing with the cotton business in a just and fitting manner, were pronounced excellent. It was resolved with great enthusiasm, to unite forces for the fostering and regulating of the cotton Import Trade, thereby, creating for Bremen, a great Cotton market, and for the spinners, an easier way of obtaining their raw material.

Six spinners joined the Board of Directors of the "Bremen Cotton Exchange".

The German Spinners Unions were now united with the Bremen Cotton Exchange, but, in the course of time, Swiss and Austria-Hungarian spinners followed suit. Through this fusion, "The Bremen Cotton Exchange" gained greatly in importance, influence and business activity, so that it stood on equal terms with the great foreign Exchanges.

At many meetings, spinners and merchants have peacefully sat at the same Board table, although the interests of both groups are frequently opposed to each other. Now and then, this has been apparent, but on the principle that good reasons must give way to better ones, differences of opinions were settled after proper discussion. Mutual understanding and a determination to pay due respect to the interests of the other party, have always been the leading spirit of the meetings. To-day, it stands beyond any doubt that through this fusion, great benefits have accrued to both parties, and to the far sighted men, who brought this about, great honor, praise and veneration are due.

In the following we give a few figures concerning the number of Members and the activity of the Bremen Cotton Exchange:

Year	Members	Arbitrations		Appeals	
1887	184	300 446	bales	29 642	bales
1892	253	653 567	"	70 340	"
1897	356	1 089 956	"	67 048	"
1902	449	1 295 441	"	63 692	"

1907	673	2 396 128	"	208 402	"
1912	717	2 554 284	"	315 597	"
1913	719	2 165 657	"	245 576	"
1920	610	405 058	"	b80 698	"
1921	663	1 041 608	"	215 066	"

We cannot possibly conclude this chapter, without drawing attention to the fact, that if the commerce has reached its present greatness by its own endeavours, the industry is fully entitled to an equal share of praise.

The German cotton industry had to pass through many a hard fight. There was a time, when German goods were deemed inferior, mainly for the reason that they were not known. The German Export Trade owes something like an apology to the Industry, for the poor support it gave at first to the exertions of the Manufacturers, to create a market for their goods in foreign countries. It took a long time before German goods were appreciated in foreign markets, but, eventually, they gained for themselves a high class reputation. The "Bremen Cotton Exchange", views with pride, the success of their fellow members of the Industry.

FINANCIAL ITEMS.

In those days, when the world spoke of the five "Great Powers", money was called the sixth "Great Power" and that with full right. It is a fact, that money means power, and that in a wider sense of the word than is generally accepted. The power of a state is limited, the power of money is unlimited, it is international. It seems ever to rejuvenate and augment itself, and it constantly draws bigger multitudes under its sway. A man who is a power in financial circles, plays his role in the world. England owes its enormous influence in politics and national economy to money. There have been other countries possessing great riches, but the working, creating and ruling capital, was English.

Previous to the English, German tribes were known on the sea. Daring mariners left our shores, and did a thriving business in all parts of the adjoining seas, where they founded settlements in the northern waters, and on the Baltic. How is it, that Germany has not gained riches, and why has it not participated in the treasures of the world, which, up to a few hundred years ago, were lying open to everybody? For the most part the unfavorable geographical position is to blame. On all sides, hemmed in by foreign countries, it had to suffer wars upon wars. A hundred years ago, Germany might still have had a chance to gain for itself a position in the world, but, at that time, it was lying in the dust, bleeding from a thousand wounds. The wars, which Napoleon waged against the German states, had reduced it to a poverty stricken country. All stamina seemed to have disappeared through the Napoleonic reign, the wars themselves and the contributions to the same, which the enemy mercilessly exacted, brought about a condition, which stifled all enterprise, and reduced the people to misery. Deep thought, poetry and music had to take the place of bodily welfare.

In their poverty, the inhabitants could not grasp the advantages offered to other nations. Under these conditions, England gained the mastery over half of the globe, politically, and in an economic sense. The colonies provided vast supplies, which were cleverly exploited, riches increased, business relations with the European Continent were opened and enlarged, and one fine day, England was the general provider to the Continent for nearly everything required. The extension of Trade was closely followed by the development of the Banking system, which, after all, may be called a branch of the trade. In the colonies, English banks were established, and every ton of rice or grain, every pound of cotton or spice, had to be paid through the intermediary of the banker, who, of course, derived a profit from the transactions.

When 50 years ago, Germany awakened from its long impotence, her citizens were received, without prejudice, all over the world, and no obstacles were placed in the way of their diligence. This fact, we wish gladly and thankfully to record. Many Germans were successful in gaining a firm footing in the English Colonies, as well as in America, and to attain there important positions. They formed a link between their home country and the centres of trade and finance. Valuable services were rendered by them to the German trade, but London remained the Banker of the world, and when an industry began to grow in Germany, it was, in many cases, the English, who furnished the first capital. When the cotton market started to develop in Bremen, most of the financing was done by English bankers, anyhow at first. Later on, German Banks participated, and it is greatly to their credit, that they showed such great interest and understanding for the requirements of that trade. In the year 1871, the first German Bank of importance opened its doors in Bremen, and others followed, as the trade expanded.

The cotton trade remained, in a certain measure, true to the English banks, while the other branches of commerce worked mostly through German banks, and a great incentive was given to this, by the fact, that American bankers considered German money equal to the American and English values.

How do we pay for the cotton, which we import?

The planter receives the purchase price from the shipper, through any one of the numerous banks in the South. Of course, we cannot give the actual dollars to the shipper, consequently, he or his banker has to advance them for a short period. Before the war, we opened a credit with English or German banks, in favor of the shipper, a so-called reimbursement credit, by which he could recover his advanced purchase price. When opening this credit, we took care, however, to have proof that the goods, for which we intended to pay, were certain to reach us eventually. We made the condition, that, against the reimbursement credit, the shipping documents were to be delivered. Against delivery of these documents, the shipper drew a draft upon our bankers, discounted the same, and the matter was settled. Now the bank was in possession of the documents, and by accepting the draft, had guaranteed to pay the purchase price. The position between the bank and ourselves, was cleared in various ways, which depended upon private arrangements. We, as cotton importers, had to receive the purchase price from the consumer in the interior, before we could satisfy our bank. As the sale of the goods could not always be effected promptly, we remained debtors to the bankers for the purchase price, while they were in possession of the goods or the documents. The settlement of transactions of this kind, requires a certain amount of trust and confidence, which the bankers have to grant to the merchants, on the other hand, they have their security in the value of the goods in their keep. The banks have always given a full measure of trust to the Bremen cotton trade, while the commerce has made every arrangement to safeguard the interests of the bankers. In this connection, we mention the establishment of the "Bremer Lagerhaus-Gesellschaft" which was founded in 1877, through their Agency the bank obtained, in a simple form, the security of the cotton itself. The hypothecation of goods against an overdraft on the bank, was new in those days, but later, it became common practice, and the old established forwarding houses made similar arrangements to those of the Bremer Lagerhaus-Gesellschaft. It became the custom to issue warrants against the cotton stored. The warehouse owners were, thereby, obliged to keep the cotton, until the holder of the warrant gave it free.

With growing trade, the co-operation of the banks increased considerably, and for a long period, business was satisfactorily settled, but the war caused here, like everywhere else, a certain amount of confusion. The settlement with the German banks was easy, but it was impossible, during the long period of the war, to let that cotton remain untouched, which was hypothecated in favor of foreign banks. Thus, a peculiar position in law was created, between the warrant holder and the previous owners of the cotton. The settlement of these questions lies with the respective committees of the peace commission.

The financial treatment of the import business after the war, is vastly different from previous methods. The American bankers play a far more prominent part, as the German importer pays in dollars on arrival of the goods in port, and he has to buy the dollars at a rate of exchange, which is subject to the vagaries of the Stock Exchange.--Recently a moderate credit has been given to the importer, but the further development of affairs is uncertain.

BUSINESS IN FUTURES.

Cotton is sold to a large extent for distant delivery, but "future" transactions are only those which are concluded on a specified "future" exchange, under the rules and regulations of that particular exchange. Here be it mentioned, that the Bremen Cotton Exchange is no exchange within the meaning of the law. It has no regular hours of attendance, nor has it special rules regulating the business in "futures". The important "future" exchanges are Liverpool and New-York, and in a lesser degree, Havre, Alexandria and New Orleans. Within the specified hours of the "future" markets, large quantities of cotton contracts change hands. There, buyers and sellers are constantly in attendance, and it requires only a nod of the head to conclude a contract for thousands of bales. The Rules, referring to "futures", do not differ essentially from those governing the general trade, for it must be borne in mind, that all "future" contracts demand the delivery of actual cotton. Nobody can escape this duty, if he has sold futures, he must deliver, unless he buys the contract back before it falls due, or vice versa, which, of course, refers also to any ordinary delivery contract. In fact, all transactions for delivery are settled either by previous transfer or by fulfilment. It is noticeable how the stocks in New-York increase or decline, in accordance with the tenders, against "futures". No doubt, the great majority of the dealers intend to close their contracts before they fall due, and the opportunity to do this, presents itself every minute. In this, the "future" markets offer a great advantage, or, if you like, a great temptation. In former days, the dealing in "futures" had no legal protection in Germany, and nowadays only under certain assumptions. Dealing in futures came within the gaming act, and claims arising therefrom, were not actionable. The Bremen Cotton Exchange has never accepted this view, but has constantly fought against it, for very good reasons. The following explanation will make it clear, that, as far as cotton is concerned, the trading in futures is of great economic importance, and not practised for snatching easily earned profits.

HEDGES.

A great market has the duty to adapt itself to all the requirements of the Trade, and these are ever changing. For instance, new districts are opened for commercial enterprise, new methods of doing business develop, bringing increased activity in their train, and all this, has to be regulated or arranged for.

Many things did not bother us in the past, as the following few questions will show:

How can we, without risk of the market, sell cotton in Spring, which will only be grown in Autumn?

How can a planter sell the cotton which he has picked, when there are no buyers at the moment?

How can a manufacturer protect himself against a decline in the price of cotton, while his goods are being prepared for the market?

How can a manufacturer accept orders for late deliveries, without possessing the cotton?

How can an importer take advantage of the great quantity of offers, which flood the market, during the first few months of the gathering of the crop?

To anybody in the cotton trade, these questions present no difficulties, but, for the outside world, be it mentioned, that it is the "future" market that furnishes the means to overcome these apparent anomalies. It is the "future" contract, which eliminates the risk of the market from the carefully managed cotton business.

Anybody who sells new crop cotton, buys a "future" contract as provisional cover, it is then immaterial to him, whether the market advances or declines. His actual sale price is the stipulated price, and the differences which arise from the "future" contract, are added or deducted. A planter, who cannot sell his cotton for the moment, sells the equivalent amount of "futures". A bank takes charge of the cotton and the "future" contract, and pays the price of the day. When the cotton is finally sold, the bank is reimbursed by receiving the then existing price of the day: plus or minus the differences on the "future" contract.

A spinner finds himself, now and then, in the position that he cannot effect sales against his production. With a decline in prices, mostly, the cessation of the demand coincides. By selling a "future" contract, he can safeguard himself. When the demand is brisk, a spinner may find himself obliged to book orders, although the time for buying the raw material is not propitious. Here also, the "futures" give the necessary assistance.

The receipts of cotton are naturally biggest in the first few months of the new season. Should an importer miss this opportunity of acquiring most desirable cotton? No, he can buy, with impunity, as much cotton as he considers advisable, for against each purchase, he can put out a provisional sale of "futures". In the cotton trade therefore, two transactions are frequently coupled. The main transaction, is the trading in the actual article, while the accompanying "futures", are a safety measure against the fluctuations of the market. This combination of actual cotton and "futures", is called a "Hedge"--the origin of this name is obscure. The "hedge" is a peculiarity of the cotton trade, it may even be called, its life condition. The supreme Court of Law has, in many decisions, upheld this condition. The endeavours of the cotton trade have always been directed towards the minimising of the market risk, and for this reason, "futures" have always played an important part in cotton business.

What are the forces which put life into the "future" market? The world's trade is large, and every minute will find people, who, in the pursuance of legitimate interests, buy or sell. When both groups are fairly equal, the market is steady, while a decline or an advance is caused by a preponderance of one over the other; finally, this adjusts itself again, by the fact, that a rapid advance will produce sellers and vice versa. A further element in the market, is the "jobber", whose main object is to take advantage of the small fluctuation caused by chance, but we must not forget the big speculators. By these, we do not mean those despicable people who aim to snatch a profit, and who, on having to face a loss, plead the gaming act. Experience and force of circumstances have, luckily, driven these parasites almost out of the market. But we do mean those big operators, who having weighed carefully "the pros and cons" of the situation, cause the great "bull" or bear movements.

TECHNICALITIES.

For those who wish to obtain information concerning the cotton trade from this pamphlet, certain subjects are here elaborated, which were, so far, only indicated in connection with other explanations.

Of first importance are the shipping documents, which consist of bills of lading and insurance certificates. There are three kinds of bills of lading: Port Bills of Lading, Custody Bills of Lading, and Through Bills of Lading. The first must be signed by the captain of the steamer, who has undertaken to carry the goods, or by a duly authorized shipping agent. They are, therefore, an absolute guarantee on the part of the ship, to deliver the goods to the holder of the bill of lading. Unfortunately, this obligation is frequently restricted by the insertion of certain inconspicuous clauses. The "custody bills of lading" are signed by a shipping agent, they acknowledge receipt of the goods, and promise the forwarding in due course. In order to obtain equal value with the "port bill of lading," they should, later on, be supplemented by a so-called "master's receipt", which is an acknowledgment by the captain, that he has actually accepted the goods for forwarding, in accordance with the conditions of the custody bill of lading. They are used when the goods have arrived at the port, previous to the ship.

The "through or railway" bills of lading, oblige the railway companies to forward the goods from a place in the interior of America, to their destination. A master's receipt is not necessary, but desirable, as it is an easy means of ascertaining by which steamer the goods are coming forward. At one time, "through or railway bills of lading" were not a properly valid document, as the railway companies were not in duty bound to forward the goods. Now, however, a change in the American Law binds the companies to this duty.

The "Insurance certificate" confirms, that the goods have been insured on the terms of an insurance policy, which remains in America, and in case of claims, it has the same documentary value as the policy itself. When "total loss", "general average" or "particular average" occur, claims on the insurer can be made, which must be substantiated in the port of discharge.

Any claim, referring to difference in quality or loss in weight, has to be made on receiving the goods, and the complaint has to be lodged within a certain specified time. On these points, the Bremen Cotton Exchange has specific rules which are easily understood.

If one party to a purchase or sale contract goes by default, the other party is obliged to send in their claim within the time stipulated by the rules of the Bremen Cotton Exchange, this is most important, as the non-observance may mean the loss of any right to claim. The method in which these claims are made up, is easily seen from the Rules of the Bremen Cotton Exchange.

If one party suspends payment, all unfulfilled contracts are immediately settled, without any action of the other party. The obligation to take or make delivery ceases, and, instead of this, the difference in price is fixed which exists between the date of contract, and the time when payment was suspended. These differences in price are put to account between the parties concerned. It can thus easily happen, that the solvent concern has to pay a considerable amount to the other party, through whose fault the contract was not carried out, and yet, this constitutes no loss to the paying party, as they can at once cover themselves at the existing prices. The advantage of this procedure lies in the fact, that the solvent concern is not left in uncertainty, whether their contracts will be fulfilled or not, while, otherwise, this decision would rest with the liquidators, who, according to Common Law, are not obliged to declare themselves, until the stipulated time for delivery has been reached.

Of great importance in the cotton trade is the business for future delivery, and that in a two-fold form. All transactions in "futures" are governed by the stringent rules of the respective Exchanges, which refer, particularly, to the price differences caused by the fluctuations in the market, and the safeguarding of the interests thus created.

Indirectly, every buyer comes frequently into contact with the "future" business, because, for years past, the importing of cotton has not been done at fixed prices, but at so many points "on" or "off" certain "futures" in New-York, for instance, a purchase is made of "goodmiddling" October/November shipment at 200 points "on" December, or lowmiddling at 200 points "off". At any period up to the time of shipment, or even of arrival of the cotton, the buyer can elect to fix the price on the market of the following day. Should then December in New-York stand at 20 cents, the price for "goodmiddling" would be 22 cents or 18 cents for "lowmiddling".

Very peculiar is the "hedge" business, to which reference has been made, and it might be advisable to give a few examples as an explanation.

A spinner is obliged to buy cotton to prevent stoppage of his mill, a sale of yarn is impossible for the moment and he decides on a "hedge" transaction. He buys "goodmiddling" at 22 cents, and sells at the same time in New-York 200 December "futures" at 20 cents. Later on, the market advances to 22 cents, and at this price the spinner covers his "future" contract, thereby, losing 2 cents. The purchase price of his 200 bales is now not 22 but 24 cents. As the movements of cotton and cotton products run on parallel lines, he has the same chance, for the sale of his production, on the basis of 24 cents, as he had at 22 cents. He gained a longer period to effect a favorable sale, while the chances of the market remained the same. It would have made no difference had the market declined to 18 cents, with a consequent gain of 2 cents, instead of a loss of 2 cents. The cotton would then have cost 20 cents, but this would have been no advantage to him, as the opportunity for selling his yarns would also have been on the basis of 20 cents.

A spinner sells his yarns for a distant delivery, at that moment, however, it does not suit him to buy the cotton, he prefers to cover himself in futures, and therefore buys 200 bales December "futures" in New-York at 20 cents. He has calculated that the sale price of his yarns allows him to pay 24 cents for goodmiddling. He watches the market for a favorable opportunity to buy "goodmiddling", he succeeds in buying 200 bales at 300 "on" December. On arrival of the 200 bales, he fixes the price with his seller, now he must be careful to liquidate his "future" contract at the same moment. Both are done at 18 cents, and he loses 2 cents on his "futures". The cotton, however, costs him 18 cents, plus the 300 points "on", equal to 21 cents, he therefore makes a profit of 3 cents on the calculated purchase price of 24 cents, from this are to be deducted, the 2 cents loss on the "futures", remaining, one cent net profit. The fluctuations of the market had nothing to do with this profit, which he had, so to say, in his pocket right from the commencement, as he had sold his yarns on the basis of 24 cents for cotton, with "futures" at 20 cents, in fact, he bought his cotton at 300 "on" for goodmiddling, with the value of "futures" at 20 cents, which equals 23 cents. The hedge business, therefore, does away with the market risk, now in what consists its value? The profit on cotton does not lie in the fluctuations of the market, one has to look for it elsewhere. The chances of profit-making are to be found for the merchant in judicious buying, while, for the manufacturer, they consist in the lucrative production of his finished articles.

The merchant requires for advantageous buying, far reaching connections and a wide spread organisation, he has to survey the entire field of cotton production, he must watch for every opportunity where cotton is pressed for sale, he must know which district has grown the qualities mostly preferred, in short, he has to keep himself extremely well posted. The consumer has to work with the same tension, to find the devious ways which lead to a profitable result in his business. Hardly ever do big profits stare one in the face, and should a particular good opportunity arise, it never lasts long, as everybody wishes to participate in it, which, of course, spoils the best chance. For the common welfare, competition tends to reduce the prices of everything to the lowest possible level, that is the natural course of events. Occasional deviations are simply exceptions, that, according to the old proverb: "prove the rule".

What is the technical value of a market?

The most pressing requirement for a spinner is a big supply, and this, naturally, collects in a big market. The manifold demands which a spinner places upon the quality, can only be satisfied by a great selection. Given a good supply, one of the main conditions of the industry has been fulfilled. An active market has a further calling, it regulates the prices, and, thereby, enables the industry to buy the raw material at a figure, warranting a successful competition in the trade of the world.

MARKET ACTIVITY
IN BREMEN.

Future transactions, of course, entail certain expenses, which constitute something of a burden on the running business, while economy is a necessity for every mercantile enterprise. Out of this, originated the desire to establish a "future" market in Bremen. People felt sure that it would greatly assist the development of the market, to be able to trade in "futures" within their own portals. A certain amount of ambition may also have lent its weight. The establishment took place, though, not under the auspices of the Bremen Cotton Exchange, but in the form of an independent society. Early in 1914, the market commenced its activities, and it was soon found, that all expectations were realised, and even surpassed. The clearing house, which was started simultaneously, fulfilled all requirements. The business with the spinners had now a foundation, which answered all demands of modern times. Covering transactions, which previously were cabled to New-York and Liverpool, could be executed here every minute within business hours. Where orders from spinners were concerned, the whole transaction could be done by telephone. The "future" market blossomed out in such a way, that no fears were entertained for its successful future.

The coping stone had been set on the edifice of the Bremen Cotton Market.

With the growth of the industry in Germany, the Bremen cotton trade expanded, and the business with the surrounding countries grew in proportion. Russia, Poland, Austria-Hungary, Switzerland, Italy, Holland and Belgium, all became faithful customers, and the Bremen Cotton Exchange hummed with activity. Here, was the centre of all the efforts to provide the consumer with the desired material at the lowest prices. Every evening, at a late hour, when the last news from America had arrived, a flood of telegrams carried advantageous offers down to the smallest and most distant places on the Continent. Not only the cotton spinner, but also the weaver, the printer and the wholesale dealer took an interest in the Bremen offers, like clockwork operated the business intercourse between the cotton factor and the cotton consumer.

THE WAR.

The Bremen Cotton Exchange has never occupied itself with politics, but, of course, the members could not help taking serious notice of occurrences which shook the world's foundation. Together, with the expansion of business, grew also a political apprehension. France was lending milliards upon milliards to the Russian Czardom, with the express condition, that the money had to be expended in preparation for a war against Germany. One saw, that France gave Egypt to England, although it did not own it, on the other hand, England ceded Marocco to France, without having any sovereign right over that country. That Germany had interests in both places, was overlooked. The English newspapers, so widely read in Bremen for their business news, brought articles upon articles, picturing the dangers of a German Invasion. In the most lurid of colors, the cruelties of the war were painted, that was supposed to threaten England, and all this, for no other purpose, than to inflame the passions of the English people.

What did the commerce do in face of these threatening symptoms?--Nothing! Without an anxious thought, people looked after their business, and showed an optimism, which to-day, is inexplicable.

On the 25th of July in 1914--after the Austria-Serbian ultimatum--careful merchants insured their afloat cotton against war risks. The big German Insurance Companies took this risk for 1/8% , let us repeat it, one eighth per cent! How was it that the insurance companies were so unconcerned? At the same time in Bremen, and at other places in Germany, many insurances were covered with English companies. Did nobody see danger ahead?

All political misgivings of those days were silenced by the feeling, that to think of war was monstrous and to believe in war, an impossibility, on account of the highly developed economic relations which connected all countries.

Yet the war came! At the outbreak, many cargoes of cotton owned by Bremen merchants were afloat, and many "future" contracts were open in the Liverpool market. Later on, the cargoes were taken by the enemy, and the Liverpool contracts were liquidated, in accordance with a certain system, but without the consent of the other parties to the contract, and without reservation of their rights. Bremen had a considerable stock of cotton at the commencement of the war, consequently was in a position to supply the German cotton mills for a long time. If proof had been needed to show the advantage of having an important cotton market in Bremen, the war would have furnished it. The cotton trade was not satisfied to deal only with the existing supply, but did its very utmost to secure fresh imports, and was successful, by means and ways hitherto unknown, to bring considerable quantities of cotton into Germany, where it was of great service.

The Cotton Exchange does not trade, but under the war-conditions and in the knowledge of being the centre of commerce and industry, a courageous attempt was made. At the instigation of the Exchange, commerce and the spinners of Germany and Austria-Hungaria united, to give a bid for one million bales of cotton to the Americans. Cotton was no contraband of war, and America was neutral, so no difficulties seemed to be in the way of executing this plan. The buyer was prepared to pay the price which the Americans might demand, and the goods were to be paid in hard cash dollars. Yet the offer was not accepted, although America had sufficient reason to seek an outlet for the big crop it had grown, and that nobody wanted under the war conditions. Politics were too mighty for the reasons of commerce!

After a while, all connections ceased with America. The Bremen Cotton Exchange and the cotton trade were at a stand-still. Now and then, the Exchange tried to place their establishment at the disposal of the trade in substitutes, but only with moderate success. To build up a lasting trade in substitutes was as impossible as it was to find a market for the substitutes, when once cotton began to appear again.

THE RE-OPENING
OF THE MARKET.

After the armistice, the possibility presented itself again, of supplying the German cotton industry with raw material. The government, however, made certain stipulations under which the import might be carried on, but no hymn of praise can be sung about them. Notwithstanding all difficulties, cotton found its way into the country, and when, finally, all government measures were cancelled, the legitimate business was restarted. All round the Bremen market, competition had grown. Rotterdam made great exertions to push Bremen aside, even Copenhagen made similar endeavours. A few American firms, which were hostile to Germany, did their best to circumvent Bremen. These efforts, however, were not crowned with success, Bremen regained its position. It has been shown that the natural development through many years, cannot be killed and artificially replaced. The manifold relations, started in peace-time, of personal or business character, showed their value. The economic life flows through a great network of channels, should these be artificially closed, they will re-open again of their own accord, as soon as the barriers have been removed. During the war, the German cotton industry either stood still, or worked only with a small percentage of its machinery. The government had husbanded the supply of cotton most carefully, so that, after an unexpectedly long war, a little was still left over. The mills which were running, displayed great assiduity in procuring and utilizing substitutes for cotton. Paper, wood, cellulose, reed and nettle fibres, and other materials were tried, some were manufactured quite extensively. During the war they did good service, but in normal times, they cannot usurp the place of cotton. After surmounting many difficulties, the German cotton industry is once more in full swing, and with it, Bremen is again the important continental cotton market. The surrounding countries buy in Bremen as of old, though some outlets are still closed, owing to political and economic reasons.

During the last three years, before the war, the import of North American cotton to Bremen averaged 2 500 000 bales, during the season 1920/21, it reached 1 200 000 bales, and in 1921/22, 1 500 000 bales, the decline, against the former years, is caused, partly, by the disappearance of some outlets, and partly, by the shorter working day.

AMERICAN CROPS
AND CONSUMPTION.

The activity of the "Bremen Cotton Exchange" depends, to a large extent, upon the import figures, and these again are under the influence of the various crops. In America, big crops alternate with small ones, the cause for this diversity is to be found in the climate conditions, and also in the ruling range of price. High prices stimulate an extensive planting and a careful cultivation of the ground, while low prices have the contrary effect. The crop figures from 1872-1914, were ascending, an occasional decline was made good later on.

The following figures will make this clear.

American crops:

1872	3 650 000	bales
1875	4 302 000	"
1878	4 745 050	"
1881	5 136 000	"
1884	5 477 000	"
1887	6 884 000	"
1891	8 940 000	"
1894	10 025 000	"
1898	10 985 000	"
1901	9 749 000	"
1904	13 697 000	"
1907	11 326 000	"
1910	11 966 000	"
1913	14 614 000	"
1914	16 738 000	"
1915	12 013 000	"
1916	12 664 000	"
1917	12 345 000	"
1918	12 817 000	"
1919	11 921 000	"

| 1920 | 13 711 000 | " |
| 1921 | 8 000 000 [1] | " |

[1] estimated.

The reverse, which the production suffered since 1914, is remarkable, it is largely accounted for, by the want of artificial manure. German potash could not be obtained, and this was largely used by all cotton states, with the exception of Texas, Louisiana, Mississippi, Arkansas, which do not require that kind of fertilizer. In addition, the boll weevil has become a dreaded enemy of the cotton plant. The insect world produces quite an army of little fiends, that viciously attack and reduce the crop, many have disappeared, but the boll weevil is, at present, the arch-enemy; it is a small beetle which bores into the bolls to deposit its eggs there.

The following figures give the distribution of the American crops.

	Export from America to		Total in thousands	Taken by American Spinners (in thousands	Percentage of the crop used by the
	Great Britain	Continent, Japan etc.			
	in thousands of bales		of bales	of bales)	U.S.A.
1871/72	1 474	483	1 957	1 097	37
1874/75	1 833	841	2 674	1 201	31
1877/78	2 047	1 309	3 356	1 496	31
1880/81	2 832	1 733	4 565	1 938	29
1883/84	2 485	1 432	3 917	1 877	33
1886/87	2 704	1 741	4 445	2 088	32
1890/91	3 345	2 446	5 791	2 640	30
1893/94	2 861	2 371	5 232	2 291	30

1896/97	3 022	2 957	5 979	2 792	32
1900/01	3 050	3 488	6 538	3 547	34
1903/04	2 577	3 455	6 032	3 935	39
1906/07	3 750	4 614	8 364	5 005	37
1909/10	2 430	3 778	6 208	4 256	40
1912/13	3 604	5 176	8 780	5 389	38
1913/14	3 419	5 447	8 866	5 503	38
1914/15	3 798	4 571	8 369	6 088	40
1915/16	2 866	3 185	6 051	6 810	53
1916/17	2 888	3 076	5 764	6 914	55
1917/18	2 247	2 179	4 426	7 073	59
1918/19	2 621	3 025	5 646	5 460	48
1919/20	3 062	3 300	6 362	6 131	50
1920/21	1 583	3 771	5 353	4 914	48
1921/22	1 946	4 586	6 532	6 308	50

From these statistics the important lesson to be learnt, is, that America has surpassed all other countries in the growth of the cotton industry. Fifty years ago, and later, America used only about 30% of the crop for home consumption, while now, it requires more than half. Equally remarkable is also the rapid growth of Japan. For many decades after 1872, Japan used hardly any American cotton, but in 1913, it took 465 000 bales; in 1920 780 000 bales; in 1921: 600 000 bales, and the estimate for 1922, is 800 000 bales. Besides this, a great many other descriptions are spun there. The use of East Indian cotton is even greater than that of American, and it reached two thirds of East India's consumption, thus placing Japan, after America and England, in the third place of cotton consuming countries. During the first half year of 1921, it has even outdone America and England, because these two countries were in the throes of a crisis.

For many decades, England had almost a monopoly for providing Asia, and the rest of the world, with cotton goods, and required a corresponding amount of raw material, but now, it has lost that position. Grave concern is felt in England, as well as in the whole of Europe, regarding the future of the cotton industry, as it seems impossible to prevent a further expansion in America and Japan, besides that, there is the growing menace of the boll weevil, which many people consider an unwelcome guest, that has come to stay.

Amongst the other cotton growing countries, Brazil perhaps, offers the best prospect, on account of the great interest taken there in the cultivation of the cotton plant, also, the Argentine gives rise to some hope.

BREMEN'S POSITION
IN COMPARISON TO THE RIVAL MARKETS.

The following figures are intended to show how the imports of
Bremen, and its consequent importance, have grown in comparison
to the great rival markets of Liverpool and Havre:

	The Import was to		
	Bremen	Liverpool	Havre
	in 1000	in 1000	1000
	bales	bales	bales
1880/81	452	2 843	543
1883/84	422	2 470	465
1886/87	493	2 694	471
1890/91	911	2 314	525
1893/94	832	2 732	578
1896/97	1 213	2 683	672
1900/01	1 546	2 478	711
1903/04	1 757	2 081	690
1906/07	2 083	3 251	863
1909/10	1 760	2 089	948
1912/13	2 216	3 066	1 001
1913/14	2 619	2 903	1 021
1919/20	385	2 477	555
1920/21	1 279	1 525	583

There are not exact statistics before 1880, however, Bremen's year-
ly import will have been 2-300 000 bales. From small beginnings,
quite a creditable result has been reached, that is worthy of some
consideration.

History frequently chronicles the decay of some once flourishing
commercial centre, and nobody knows to-day, the exact reason.
Was it an opportunity missed? Of such, no records are kept in the
book of time. Should anybody compile a history of lost opportuni-

ties, it might easily require a bigger volume, than that needed for the story of opportunities taken at the crucial moment.

The river, on which Bremen is situated, was so heavily silted up, that sometimes in Summer, one could wade through it; no sea-going vessel could reach the town. Under these circumstances, the opportunity of establishing a cotton market in Bremen might easily have been missed. The trade which was indigenous to Bremen passed, in the second half of the 19th century, through a period of transition. The shipping business from olden times, a main stay of Bremen's commerce, had to adapt itself to more modern requirements. The small vessels hitherto used, had to make way for bigger ones, the steamship had entered into the world's traffic. There was hardly a proper connecting link with the interior, no water ways existed, and the efficiency of the railways was extremely poor. Surely, these were not conditions that cried for the opening of a market centre. Yet it was established, it grew and blossomed into success.

Was this chance or method?

We owe many thanks to the State of Bremen for its co-operation, for, with astounding energy, this small state undertook to build a sea-port in Bremen town. This necessitated the deepening of the river "Weser", to which work the neighbouring states lent no help, but rather, placed difficulties in the way.

This grand work deserves an essay of its own, on account of its influence on the commercial, political and economic position of Bremen. Here only, be it mentioned, that the furtherance of the cotton trade was a constant stimulus to this great plan. The authorities and the representatives of the trade were in the best harmony, and the most perfect arrangements were made for the dealing with cotton. Great practical knowledge and experience was shown, in settling the question of how to raise the interests and amortization needed for the vast expenditure, and of how much the trade could bear without crippling it. The state furnished the capital for the building of great warehouses, and within a number of years their cost was paid off, as planned. In this way, Bremen became equipped with all modern requirements for the handling and storing of cotton, which, even to-day, are unsurpassed. The port has the highest reputation for the quick and painstaking unloading and dispatching of cotton cargoes.

The co-operation of the banks has already been mentioned, but we do not deem it superfluous to repeat, that without capital, no enterprise can be effectively launched, and all roads to successful completion are barred. Fifty years ago Bremen was poor in capital. What existed of riches, and was not needed in business, was, by preference, locked up in American securities, very little was left liquid for the Cotton Trade, although big amounts were needed to handle the import of cotton. Credit is not given by merely asking for it, only he is entitled to it, who is sure that he can fulfil his obligation. To incur debts, trusting to luck to pay back, is bad policy. It is unfair dealing to accept goods on credit in the hope that their sale will leave a profit, this is only permissible, when sufficient capital is in existence to pay for the goods, even though a loss takes the place of the expected profit. As these views dominated the trade, close connections could be started with the banks. State and banks have greatly helped the growth of the Bremen cotton trade, besides them, however, the assistance of many others must be gratefully acknowledged. Most particular reference has to be made to the forwarding trade. With admirable energy, the forwarding houses made all arrangements for the careful and expeditious handling of the technical part of the cotton trade. Right from the beginning, they worked on the principle of trustworthiness and reliability, well knowing, that only by these, a mutual confidence between all parties could be established. The great trust shown, alike by shippers and receivers, to the Bremen Forwarding firms, has made the dealing so easy and satisfactory. The post and telegraphic authorities have likewise been imbued with good will towards the needs of commerce, thereby assisting considerably the furtherance of trade. The harmonious cooperation of so many powerful allies, enhanced the value of the work done by the cotton market itself, though, never for a moment, must the diligent work slacken, lest the budding tree should stop growing. Anybody engaged in the cotton business has to be at his post every minute, always ready to take a given opportunity. Exact information concerning the conditions in America, as well as personal connections in that country, are of great value. It is characteristic of the German merchant to follow up a business once he has commenced it, and this close attention, from early youth to ripe old age, has contributed materially to the success of the Bremen cotton trade.

FLUCTUATIONS IN PRICES.

In the Spring of 1921, the following conversation might have been overheard between an American and a German.

A.: You see the consequences of the war are worse for the victor than for the vanquished.

G.: Only apparently, and for the moment. The future, I fear, will teach us something different.

A.: Nobody can look into the future. At the present minute, we witness the biggest economic collapse that the world has ever seen, all countries suffer from it, except Germany. All states had made preparations for peace, now the stored up goods are lying there and nobody wants them, not even Germany. We thought, that Germany, bare of everything, would swallow anything.

G.: The reason is, that Germany cannot pay. Her gold and tangible gold values have been taken from her. Why do not the other countries buy? Their peace production has been lying idle for years, consequently, the shelves must be fairly empty.

A.: Quite right, but prices have risen to an unreasonable height. During the war, a most wasteful regime prevailed; everybody made big profits or received huge wages, and accustomed himself to a most sumptuous life. Now, vengeance is upon them, for nature does not allow herself to be ravished, nor does she present gifts for extravagant living.

G.: If prices have been driven to an unreasonable level by wasteful workings, then, a big decline in prices is the only remedy.

A.: We are in the midst of a phenomenal collapse of prices. Cotton is a barometer for all other goods. The price in America is, to-day, 11 cents, a short while ago, it was 40 cents.

G.: What does the planter say to this?

A.: The cost of production is for him this season about 25-30 cents per pound. He has worked for nothing, and besides, loses a good deal of money, as his means are small, he will be heavily in debt.

G.: And the further consequences?

A.: The planter is absolutely unable to produce a similar crop. It is the old story, when prices are too low the crop will be curtailed.

G.: We have always experienced that low prices are followed by high ones. What other consequences is this collapse in prices likely to have?

A.: All cotton goods fall in the same proportion as the raw material, this means a bad crisis for commerce and industry, and an unprecedented amount of unemployment. Besides, this collossal drop in prices has caused other very peculiar situations.

G.: Of what nature?

A.: It is well known that cotton is rarely bought at a fixed price, but generally, at the "future" price of the day on which the buyer "calls" his cotton, plus or minus the agreed upon difference for the quality bought. Now, several American houses sold low qualities, at 12.50 cents "off". At that time, "futures" were 40 cents, so that the seller calculated to receive about 27.50 cents, to-day, "futures" are 11 cents, so that, if the buyer "calls" his cotton to-day, he receives it for nothing, and can claim 1.50 cents per pound as well.

G.: Impossible! No German law would permit a buyer to demand his goods, without paying a price at all, and be justified in claiming money in addition from the seller.

A.: What decision would the Bremen Cotton Exchange give? Two possibilities are to be taken into account. If the seller has taken a "future" contract as cover, he has no loss, even if he gives the cotton for nothing, and pays 1.50 cents in addition, because the difference in the "futures" indemnifies him. But if he has no "futures", what then? to part with valuable cotton for nothing, and pay good money as well, would exceed the demands of Shylock.

G.: The "Bremen Cotton Exchange" would probably decline to adjudicate, it has the right to refer it to the ordinary law courts.

A.: A hard nut to crack for the law!

German and American agree on the following:

It is a peculiar thing that cotton has always new riddles in store for us. The fluctuations in prices are enough to drive a man mad. Woe to him, who is drawn into that maelstrom. The hedges are a safe guard against price fluctuations. The careful merchant thinks he is on solid ground, when, all of a sudden, the premium for the quality begins to rock and he wonders what is worse? the fluctuation of the "future" market, or those of the premiums. Hundreds of thousands of bales have been sold, at a premium of 10 to 15 cents for goodmiddling, to-day, the premium is 3 cents, that spells hard times for the cotton market. It is a consolation, that bad times are quickly followed by good ones, and that the darkest hour is before dawn. Cotton typifies life and death, joy and sorrow. It is like an untamed animal, it deals serious wounds, it indulges in "buck jumps", that none can foretell, nobody has ever driven it in harness. And yet, he, who deals with it quietly, carefully and pluckily, will always remain fresh and full of life.

Cotton is king!

THE EXCHANGE BUILDING.

In the year 1902, the Bremen Cotton Exchange opened the doors to its various tenants, and, as the outward appearance of a man has an influence on the impression he makes upon us, so does the building which houses the cotton trade, play its part. Previous to that date, the business of the Exchange was carried on in rented rooms, but with expanding trade, these became inadequate, and a new building was contemplated; the idea was, to make the outward appearance worthy of the importance of Bremen's cotton trade, with due consideration to the local conditions. Bremen can boast of a thousand years history, and has many fine examples of ancient architecture, notably around the market place. There you find in the rich ornate style of the renaissance, the "Rathaus" (town hall) and in another style, that however blends harmoniously, is the "Schütting" (the seat of the chamber of commerce), the "Dom" (cathedral), the "General Exchange", as well as a number of private houses of a later date. The combined appearance of these various buildings, form an imposing picture. The site for the new exchange is situated in this very neighbourhood, consequently, a building had to be designed that fitted in with the whole scheme. Prominent architects competed, and the plans that gained the first price were accepted, and commissioned for execution. Unfortunately, it was proved later on, that the choice had not been a lucky one. The architect adopted the style of the ancient "Rathaus", but the rich ornamentations of this architecture, proved its doom. Beautiful as the effect was on the smaller, gracefully built, Rathaus, yet on the ponderous building of the "Exchange", it was utterly unsuitable, and another thing the architect did not consider sufficiently: The old guild masters, with their circumspection and devotion, erected buildings to last an eternity, while now-a-days, all is hurry and scurry, the sooner the job is finished the better, as fresh orders are waiting. This may, possibly, be some excuse for the little care bestowed upon the selection of the material. The soft sandstone selected, was excellently suited to the quick sculpturing of the over-rich ornaments, nevertheless, it was a ghastly mistake to have chosen it. Ten years after the building was finished one of the decorations, loosened by the weather, fell, and killed a member of the Exchange. An examination showed that a great number of projecting stones were so weatherworn, that they

crumbled in the hand. An ugly scaffolding had to be erected to protect the street traffic. Measures were at once taken to construct the
front of the building more solidly; the most prominent experts were
asked for their advice, but the war broke out, and nothing could be
done. During the first years after the war, want of money prevented
the starting of the repairs. These had become more extensive, owing
to the revolution, when the building had been under artillery and
rifle fire. At last, however, came the propitious moment, when one
could think seriously of beginning the work. It was thought of raising half the estimated cost of 15 millions, by voluntary contributions
from the trade and the industry, and both responded nobly to the
call. But the moment the money was secured, most of it melted
quickly away, through the depreciation of the Mark. Nevertheless,
this day of the 50th anniversary sees the work in full swing, and it
will not be long, before the too richly carved front of the building
will have given place, to one of greater simplicity and nobility,
which better express the wishes of the Cotton Exchange. The interi-
or of the Exchange is entirely adapted to the needs of the business,
special attention is being paid to the light. The judging and valuing
of cotton, require a pure and clear day light, this is of such importance, that it cannot receive too much consideration. A portion of
the building is reserved for the Cotton Exchange, while the remain-
der is utilised as offices for the various cotton firms, unfortunately,
there is not room enough for all of them. It would be of great advantage, if all the firms could be housed under one roof, and plans
for this are contemplated, but when they will be executed, depends
entirely upon the economic development of the future.

WORLD-WIDE BUSINESS.

A New-York commission agent, who has connections all over the world, receives a telephonic message from Texas to sell 100 bales of "futures". At the same moment, he receives a cable to buy a 100 bales of "futures", both orders equalize each other, the execution is easy, a few words on the telephone, a cable, a letter, and the business is done. Such transactions are daily occurrences, they leave no particular impression, nor call for any deep thought. And yet, it is very interesting to probe deeply to find the origin of this business. A planter in Texas has worked hard for six months with his entire family, to raise his cotton crop. In the early days of Spring, the ground had to be cleared and ploughed to prepare it for the seed. Then comes the time of sowing, and soon afterwards, the weeds require attention. Hardly have these been uprooted, when the injurious insects make their appearance, they are destroyed by artificial means. Over and over again, the fields require most careful attention, till, at last, the cotton begins to ripen. In the broiling sun it is picked, and only then, the planter is sure about the out-turn of his crop. The prices are favorable at the moment, and he makes his calculations. For extra help, he had spent so much, and for the frugal life of his family and himself, a further amount was required, but the account was all right. If he could obtain the present price for cotton, he could pay for everything, and have a margin to the good. He decided to secure the price by giving the afore-mentioned order.

In the family of a landed proprietor in Hungary, was joyful excitement, the daughter of the house had become engaged to be married. The wedding was to take place soon, and the question of the trousseau was discussed. This, resulted in a visit to a merchant in a neighbouring town, who discovered that his stocks had run too low for the reputation of his business; at once, he gave a commission to the wholesale merchant, who, in turn, sent a considerable order to the manufacturer. Thus it goes on, till finally, the mill that spins the yarn, buys the cotton in Bremen, where the merchant cables New-York, to cover the "futures". The business, so unconcernedly done in New-York, had deep lying reasons, which never came within the vision of the commission agent. In a similar manner, the world's transactions are governed. We do not look beyond our own particular horizon, we take what the minutes bring us, without troubling our sluggish mind for the "whys" and "wherefores". Nothing, however, is done in the world's eternal circle, without cause and effect. Should our mental capacity be able to grasp every transaction in its entirety, we should see, that a never ending thread connects all of us who live and work.

When the thread is broken, disorder and confusion replace the organisation, that is as finely balanced as the delicate works of a clock, and endless trouble is required to piece the thread together again.

CONCLUSION.

The jubilee of the "Bremen Cotton Exchange" takes place at a time, when all economic conditions are in dire confusion. Never before, was the economic life, embracing all countries, so finely spun, as in our modern times, and now, the net is torn in untold places. The old Europe, predominant for over two thousand years in all spheres, lies bleeding from serious wounds, and the question is, what part will it play in the future, what will be its fate? Finally lost is the dominant position in the region of Finance. No longer does it reap the interests and means, which originated from the economic assistance it gave to countries in other parts of the globe. On the contrary, Europe, itself, has to pay interests, and within Europe, between the different countries, obstructions and impediments are heaped upon each other, to surmount them, is a work for "giants"! The only consolation is, that it is not the first time that Europe and our own Germany were in sore distress. In all previous cases, it recuperated, and rose, like a Phoenix, from the rejuvenating fire. The plague and other dread epidemics have devastated towns and countries, wars have destroyed peoples and their culture. Final ruin we see, only in cases, where discord and lack of reason have permanently come to reign.

The continued depreciation of currency in the affected countries, is one of the causes of the many grievances. No remedy has yet been discovered for it, but it must be apparent to everybody, that the most precious treasure possessed by man, is not GOLD, but "WORK"!

Work alone, however, is not in all circumstances a protection against misery. The possibility must exist to use it correctly in exchange for other goods. The overthrow of all to which we have been accustomed, is likely to cloud our vision, but, ultimately, we have to acknowledge that men and nations depend upon each other, and that, in the exchange of our earthly goods, life and the pleasures of life can be found for each individual.

Amidst all this oppression and tribulation, it is a blessing to be able to look back upon a successful past. This privilege, however, has stern duties: to keep up the traditions of the past, to adhere to the approved fundamental principles, to regain the lost, to strive and build up afresh.

With this determination, the Bremen Cotton Exchange celebrates its fiftieth anniversary.